CLAIM IT

Written By

Dr. Geneva Scott

To every child and teenager searching for hope
— may you always remember that
your circumstances do not
define your destiny.

CLAIM IT

Written By
Geneva Scott

Illustrations & Fullcover Design By
Sun Child Wind Spirit

Transcription By
Dr. Mari Michelle

Proofread By
Mylia Tiye Mal Jaza

BePublished.Org

CLAIM IT

ISBN-13: 978-0709997818   ISBN-10: 8156742060

Author Contact Info
Geneva Scott
ablessed14u@yahoo.com

Self-Publishing Associate
BePublished.Org
Chicago, IL 60602
Dr. Mary M. Jefferson
P.O. Box 8324
Jackson, MS 39284
mari@bepublished.org

First Edition.
Printed in the United States of America.
Recycled Paper Encouraged.

TABLE OF CONTENTS

DEDICATION

This book is dedicated to **Vivian Gibson**, my faithful friend who has been with me through thick and thin — one who speaks hope, listens without judgment, and reminds me to keep being the woman God called me to be.

I have lived through the criticism of others and overcome depression that once held me in bondage. I thank God for His amazing favor and for freeing me from darkness into light.

Twelve years ago, I suffered a stroke that became the turning point of my life.

In that moment, I heard God ask, *"Do you want to live or die?"* I answered, *"Lord, I want to live — but not like this."* His reply: *"Then live on."*

And that is exactly what I have done — every day since.
To God be the glory: **I am still living on.**

SPECIAL THANKS

Gone But Never Forgotten

To my beloved parents, **Mr. and Mrs. Levi Scott, Sr.**, who have gone home to be with the Lord — you will never be forgotten. You taught me that I had to make things happen for myself, and that no one else could finish what I started. Every achievement and blessing in my life reflects your strength, guidance, and love. *Out of sight does not mean out of mind.* I love you always.

Mrs. Earline Hines — A dear friend who always lifted my spirits and lived with kindness. You taught me what it means to live your best life, and I'm grateful for your constant encouragement and example.

Mr. Eddie Burleigh — You were a great inspiration both at church and at home. You made a way out of no way and offered comfort when fear tried to take over. Thank you for being a true man of God and for your caring spirit.

Dr. Don Gibson — A doctor and friend who went beyond the call of duty. You cared deeply, protected my privacy, and never gave up on me. Thank you for your patience, your gentle voice, and your faithful belief that healing begins with faith.

Thank you for everything you did and said to me. We had a unique bond. You three never said a negative word to me. You were always smiling, and always available to me! My Radiant Stars that only saw the best in me.

Other Tributes

Mrs. Valerie Noflin — A woman of strength, encouragement, and faith. Thank you for your listening ear and your growth in grace. I have watched God transform us both, and I am thankful for your sisterhood in Christ.

Mrs. Marilyn Washington Toaster — A woman filled with the Word of God. Thank you for introducing me to Jesus Christ and helping me build a personal relationship with Him. My continued walk with God began through your love and teaching.

Mrs. Shirley Wilson — A woman of peace and loyalty. You were a true friend in my time of need, standing beside me without judgment. I will always remember your quiet strength and the way you modeled faith through action.

Dr. Gwendolyn Conley Thompson — A woman of great talent and quiet wisdom. Thank you for believing in me, for encouraging me through hard times, and for reminding me that *only what you do for Christ will last.*

Mrs. Darlene Dennis — Thank you for believing in my writing, keeping me focused on my goals, and reminding me to follow what *God* wants, not what others expect. Your friendship and wisdom have meant so much.

Thank you for **Gail Tucker, Linda Chambers, Jean Frazier, Michael Smith, Minnie Erhabor, Delois Lott, Mwendaendi Lewanika,** and all the **Prayer Warriors** from **Mount Galilee M.B.**

Church Prayer Line, and from **Rev. B.K. Knott Prayer Line** — all my sisters and brothers that keep me grounded in the Word. Thank you for your participation. Remember: **"The Best is yet to come!"**

Dr. Felix Adah — Thank you for sharing your prophetic vision with me in 1999. You said I would one day hold a doctorate degree. Thirty years later, through God's grace, that vision came true. A vision that has become reality!

To **All family, mentors, teachers, and friends** — those still living and those who have gone on—who have helped shape her into the woman she is today. Through their guidance, love, and faith, a young girl who became a mother at thirteen grew into a woman who walks boldly in her purpose, giving all glory to God.

PREFACE

<u>CLAIM IT</u> is the final book in my first collection of short stories — a series written for young people struggling to find their way, to overcome hardship, and to cope with medical conditions or life decisions that shape their futures.

I have faced many difficulties, including serious medical challenges that tested her faith and perseverance. Through my work, I share lessons drawn from my own experiences and those of my students -- many of whom also faced emotional or physical struggles while in her classroom.

This third and final book follows a child who learns to trust in what his grandmother has always taught him — that faith and patience reveal God's truth in time. In discovering this for himself, he confirms that Grandma's wisdom was more than words; it was a promise fulfilled.

"Good morning," said Grandmother.

"Hello, Grandma," I answered quietly, trying not to show the storm stirring in my chest.

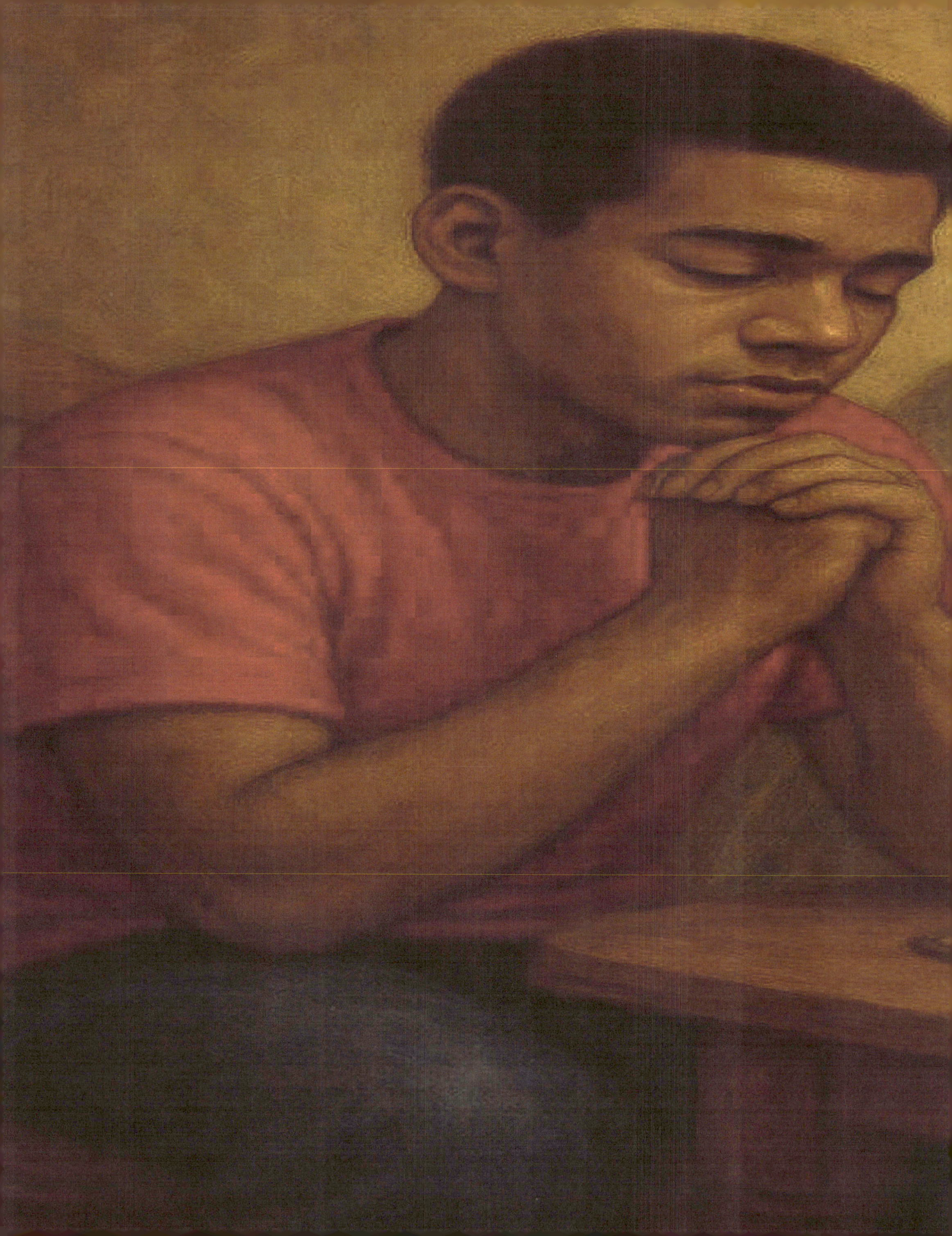

"You seem to have a lot on your mind lately, son," she said, sitting her teacup down.

She gave me a that look, and I knew she could see right through a soul.

"You've been in another world these days," she said.

"Yes, Grandma, I know those words by memory. You've told me time after time. But sometimes I don't know if I can really hear Him speaking directly to me. I hear you say, 'Just wait and be of good courage,' and that plays over and over in my head. But Grandma, my choices are so wide — I don't even know where to start. I'm getting letters every day, and I haven't even finished my senior year yet."

She nodded and said again, "Just trust and obey. God will lead you in the right direction. You must make a choice that you will be pleased with."

Later that day, my friends stopped by.

"Yo, Tunk! What's up, man?" said Jerry, grinning ear to ear.

"Nothing much," I said.

"Kyriah and I are going to a party tonight," Bryson said. "You wanna come hang out?"

I shook my head. "Nah, I'm good. I think I'll stay in and read. I've got a lot of decisions to make about my future, and I really need to think things through."

Kyriah rolled her eyes. "Boy, you always thinking. Don't you ever get tired of that? You need to live a little!"

They all laughed.

Bryson said, "Yeah, man! You always in your head. Loosen up!"

I smiled faintly. "I made that mistake once — following the crowd. It cost me everything. I went from a high place to the lowest point I could imagine. But God saw me through it. I know Grandma and her prayer partners were lifting me up all the while."

My three friends nodded and agreed.

Bryson said, "Yeah, man. I remember. You were the talk of the town back then."

"Yeah," I said quietly. "And I don't ever want to go back there. Don't follow the 'street committee,' you hear me? Don't listen to what's supposed to make you feel good or make you fit in. That's a setup for failure. I lost three years of progress because I wanted to be cool instead of wise."

We both went silent.

That night, after they left, I sat alone at the table, just thinking. I thought about Grandma's words, about my mother's prayers, about all the wrong turns I had taken.

The house was quiet. I could hear my own heartbeat. I pushed my chair back, knelt down right there on the floor, and began to pray.

"Lord, please forgive me of all my unrighteousness. Help me, Lord. I need your guidance. I need your strength. Show me the way I should go. I want to make a difference in my life."

Tears streamed down my face as I stayed there, whispering my heart to God. Then something shifted inside me — peace flooded my chest.

I lifted my hands and shouted softly, "Thank you, Lord! Thank you, thank you, thank you! You are my Savior!"

The next morning, I ran downstairs, hungry but happy. Grandma had made my favorite breakfast — cheese grits, eggs, sausage, and flapjacks.

She smiled and said, "Your sister Kamisha is here, and your mama's on her way. Your daddy too."

When everyone arrived, we all sat down together. I could barely hold it in.

Finally, I said, "I've decided — I'm joining the Army."

Kamisha gasped. "But they said you couldn't because of your feet!"

I grinned. "They approved me. I'm going to basic training."

Mama and Daddy looked at each other and smiled.

Grandma wiped a tear.

Everyone was filled with joy. Before we ate, Grandma prayed, thanking God for new beginnings.

We laughed and talked like never before. I felt lighter — like I could finally breathe. I had the blessing of the people who mattered most.

Later, Grandma said quietly, "Petition God's throne of grace, and He will give you the desires of your heart. Claim it, baby. Claim every good thing God has for you."

And I did.

A week later, my parents threw me a going-away dinner.

The restaurant was packed with family and friends.

Even folks from my daddy's side who rarely came around were actually there to celebrate with me.

We laughed and talked until morning.

Grandma didn't stay long.

But before she left, she pressed a wad of one-dollar bills in my hand and said, "Count your blessings, one by one."

I smiled. She never gave up on me.

That night, lying in bed, I thought about my school years — elementary, junior high, high school.

I remembered my daddy at my elementary graduation, waving from the back.

I remembered the day I lied about being sick just to stay home and play my Xbox.

Then, I remembered high school.

And, when I said yes to drugs and alcohol.

When I thought I was too smart to fall.

It all came crashing back — the night of prom.

The edibles I brought.

The moment my classmate Erica
collapsed on the dance floor.

The sirens, the screaming, the terror that
I had killed my friend.

Thank God she survived! But that night changed everything.

I confessed to the principal and took the blame.

My six friends stood with me — they admitted they were part of it too.

Other students even came forward.

We were all expelled from the honors class.

Out of the seven of us, four rebuilt our lives.

One girl went back to finish high school. Three of us — me included — had the military on our minds. One went straight to work. Another started doing hair.

We stayed friends. Nobody blamed anyone anymore.

We learned that bad decisions don't have to define you. What matters is what you do next.

As Grandma always said, "Don't you walk in fear or bow to pressure."

"Whatever you want to achieve!"

"Speak it, believe it, and claim it."

And now I know for sure that God is with me.

He was with me through the storm, through my shame, and through my victory.

I won't walk in fear anymore.

I won't bow to pressure.

Everything I desire, everything I dream, I will achieve because I have God – and because I will forever claim it!

THE ARTIST & ART

Dr. Geneva Scott

Dr. Geneva Scott is a native Jacksonian. She has four older brothers (Levi Jr., Robert, Michael and James) and one older sister (Mable). Geneva is the daughter of Mr. Levi Scott, Sr. and Mrs. Rosetta Scott. She has one daughter (Carmitha), two grandchildren (Adarrius and Carmesha), and one son-in-law (Arthur).

Dr. Scott attended Lanier High School where she had many difficulties, but graduated on time in 1981. She has gone beyond the norm from being a 13-year-old parent to having a Specialist Degree from Mississippi State University. She earned her Master's Degree and her undergraduate degree at Jackson State University. Her Associate's Degree was earned at Hinds Junior College. In 2025, she received two honorary doctorate degrees (PhD and Doctorate of Divinity, both in

Ministry Sciences) earned through her community service, evangelism, educational and literary contributions.

She continues to encourage others to never give up on life, their dreams, God or themselves. She urges them to always know they will be enabled to fight the good fight of faith and should try to worry less or put things off.

Dr. Scott has gone through many obstacles in her life. The most memorable would be a stroke that she experienced in 2009. She looks back on her illness as strength to accomplish many goals for today. She is one that knows that her life is truly a testimony.

In fact, she lives on the scripture that says, "I can do all things through Christ who strengthens me."

A prayer. A choice. A destiny waiting to be claimed. In **CLAIM IT**, a heartfelt and powerfully illustrated story for pre-teens and teens, Dr. Geneva Scott captures the moment every child faces — that quiet crossroad where right and wrong, purpose and temptation, meet. Meet Tunk, a bright African-American young man growing up in a world full of tough decisions: school or parties, chores or friends, faith or peer pressure.

At his grandmother's kitchen table, he whispers a prayer that will shape his life — one that carries him from confusion to courage, from uncertainty to leadership. What Tunk doesn't know is that his small prayer will echo far into his future. Through faith, focus, and discipline, he will rise to become a respected soldier, a community leader, and a man who teaches others how to claim their purpose before the world claims them.

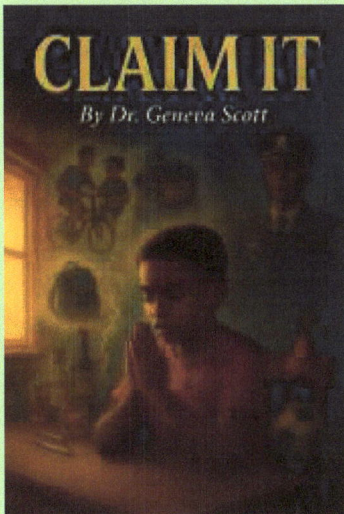

With rich, full-color illustrations inspired by classic Norman Rockwell storytelling art peppering the work, this is a message that speaks to every child's potential. Published in November 2025 with assistance from BePublished.org, it is available worldwide as a Kindle eBook and also available globally as a softcover / paperback book from online and bricks-and-mortar book resellers.

CLAIM IT reminds readers that greatness begins with a single decision to believe in something more. It's perfect for classrooms, Sunday schools, youth programs, readers ages 9 to 16 navigating life choices, and parents and mentors seeking meaningful conversations about faith, responsibility, and destiny.

Retired from the Jackson Public School system after 30 years of dedicated service, the author of **BELIEVE IT** can always remember her affirmation that she would recite with her students every morning before the school day started. Her emphasis is placed on each individual making up their mind to do as well as they could throughout the day.

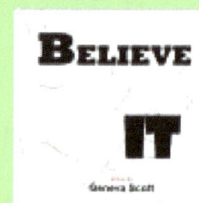

So it was with that emphasis that she had written this book, **I AM THAT I AM**. As she reflected on her illness, as well as illnesses that she has come in contact with over the years. She had made up her mind that she isn't going to allow anything to keep her from living life and living it more abundantly with Christ.

Even though, in Autumn 2025, she was still recovering from a stroke, she completed writing and quickly released **CLAIM IT** -- not allowing her illnesses to force her to give up on her dreams or life. She's presently working on completing her autobiography.

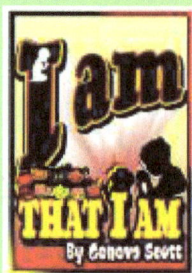

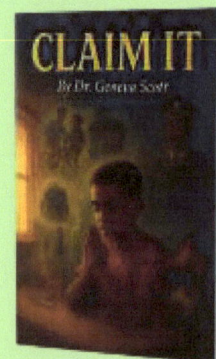

Dr. Scott is one who lives life according to the scriptures and enjoys every opportunity she has to make others smarter, wiser and happier. Despite her current illnesses, she has survived day by day and knows that she is a living testimony of how, with God's help, you can thrive no matter the circumstances. She knows that, **"I Am That I Am"** blesses us all as long as we truly **"Believe It"** and actually feel that way when we **"Claim It."**

ABlessed14U@yahoo.com